Dianne

Unheard Whispers

(Poems on growing up in an alcoholic home)

All Rights Reserved

Published By

Poets Choice ®
www.poetschoice.in

First Edition March 2022

Cover Design By Ksenija Petranovic , Serbia
Book Designed By Laura Antonioli, England
Editor - Kaneez Zehra , India

ISBN: 978-93-94020-41-2

Price

₹ 500
$ 22.5

BCID: 159-16488149

Visit www.bookcrossing.com

For the children of all ages affected by another's addiction in any form—it is not you, and it never was. You are enough, and you are beautiful, lovable, and unique. Make your life yours, and please know that you are not alone.

Table of Contents

Little Brown Bird

Carry me away with you
little brown bird.
I want to soar high in the sky.
You are free, happy.
I know. I see.
Here, I'm trapped with them—

with him.
I'll tell you a secret—he hurts me.
Oh no, it's not what you think,
little brown bird.
He doesn't mean to—I think.
But he likes it when I cry—

sometimes. I wish I could fly.
Where is your family,
little brown bird?
Do you ever cry?
I bet you don't often—

because you can fly.

Stuck

In the dark, there are secrets. They hang in the air, stuck like flies on limp tendrils of adhesive, whispered buzzing, begging for help. There you sit—in the dark—in your secrets. Why do they strengthen at night? We're so tired of pretending, hiding in the shadows—your family, your children. You're our shadow, monstrous and suffocating. We are so small, stuck in your mysteries—smothered by your substance. Bloodshot baby blues turn to dust and are carried away in a gentle breeze. You're blessed not to see the destruction. You're blessed again not to feel pain—our buzzing whispers—your family, your children. Blind and numb, you sit, oblivious to the shattered glass of our broken hearts.

Tied

The tight blue Windsor pressed into your neck.
With a grape juice stain from lunch shaped like a heart,
it's perfection, the blue, with tiny white flecks.
You wear it with pride. You're better. You're smart.

I see you hiding the clip, just so, in shame.
Worn not by the smart but those who pretend to be.
The drunks like your father who never became—
the smokers, boot-wearers—the ones who offend.

The ties live differently—*perfect, money, smart,*
better lives than ours and safer in the dark.
One day you'll be there—*all perfect—money, smart.*
Tied to a better life to leave your mark.

Never a pretender, a guy who'll never be.
From your dad's drinking, you'll now be free.

The Storm

It's safe in the dead.
Quiet and calm like the sea before a storm.
A rising tide builds and
pressure pulses.

Grazing rabbits are free in the sun.
Then, the hawk soars and strikes.
We know the answer but question its arrival,
the when and if—the storm.

Boots on the floor,
their clicking rhythmic pattern,
same pace, same steps,
ten to my door.
Four clicks on linoleum,
then quiet—
rug.
Linoleum again,
four more clicks—door.
Mine.

No time to hide.
Barbie climbs into bed,
too cool to be tucked.
Her pink shoes are neat and together
on the floor.

He has something to tell me.

He always does.
It's the same as before—
divorce.
They're getting divorced.
It doesn't hurt—anymore.

I pretend to cry so he leaves,
so he's happy.
I imagine if he were lost, gone,
if they divorced.
He's not easy to lose.

I hate myself.
"Don't leave, Dad. Don't go."
Go, please leave. Please leave us alone,
leave forever.
God forgive me.

No! I love him.
"I love you, Dad. Don't go. It will be okay."
I stroke his head.
My cheeks are wet from tears.
They stick and slide against his.

He's happy now.
He's happy that I'm sad.
Same as always.
Children crying—he is smiling,
his children.

Rhythmic clicks on linoleum
quiet again on the rug.
The sun returns and
rabbits graze.

I love you, Dad—the storm.

White Rabbit

The folding doors of the bus screech open,
kids tumble out to the curb.
A mad dash home,
welcomed with hugs and cookies.
I imagine.

1, 2, 3, 4
I count the steps to the door,
one foot in front of the other.
"One hundred twelve steps to the door.
One hundred and twelve steps to the door."
I say it twice,
always twice.

The Monday through Friday ritual.
I wonder what would happen if I didn't?
I can't risk it.

Mom's not home—he is,
in his chair in the kitchen.
A table leg is broken, splintered and sharp.
He's face down,
hand still on his cup,
the other dangles lifeless at his side.
I put my fingers close to his wanting to touch them—I don't.

The porch—an open door.
Rabbit's cage is empty!
I spin around the room.
He's gone—white rabbit.
"White rabbit," I whisper,
"Where are you?"

"White rabbit's gone. White rabbit's gone."
I say it twice, thinking it will help.
No one's here to help. No one hears.
He's lifeless.
Dead in his seat.
He dies a lot,
then comes back to life, like magic,
except not magic.

I need real magic for white rabbit.
"Real magic. Real magic."
I sit on the floor and hold his dead hand.
"Where's rabbit, Dad? Where's rabbit?"
I whimper one hundred and twelve times.
He doesn't answer,
still dead.

A million rabbits surround me.
I search for mine.
White rabbit—I know him,
he's not there.

Arms lift me and carry me to bed.
It's dark now, everything's dark.
He's alive again.
"Where's my rabbit, Dad? Where's my rabbit?"
Did you see him?

Ruined

The louder their voices,
the quieter I am.
Crawling inside myself, I can't speak
or feel.
Still, like puddle water after rain,
I can't move.

Then a crash—
a car wreck—a busted nose through the windshield,
bloody and warm.
I shake.
I twitch.
I can't move.
Something fell, maybe a picture?

Sounds of crunching glass in a frame.
I hope it's the one of all of us, ruined.
The one at the beach—
pretending.

Mr. Murray next door comes home from work.
It must be 5 o'clock.
I see him out my window, approach his wife.
His suit is without any wrinkles—perfect.

Tap tap tap.
He touches Mrs. Murray's shoulder
as she waters flowers on their porch.

She turns to him,
smiling.
He smiles back, and she pats his tie.
They kiss,
happy.

I know why Ray begged Mom for the clip-on tie when school started.
He sees Mr. Murray, too,
from his window.
There's no yelling there.
No wrinkles.

We're off to get pizza,
rushing down the steps.
Mom pulls us hurriedly,
mumbling under her breath.
We don't get pizza on all drunk nights,
just these.

The caramel, clear liquid, poison nights.
The yelling crashing ones.
The bad ones.
The bloody ones are new.
I'll ask for dessert.

Blink blink blink.
No more blood and no more smells.
The caramel, clear liquid, poison,
sour whiskey smell.
Ray cries as Mom sighs,
and we drive to get our pizza.

I try to blink away the picture
of us on the floor, under broken glass—
of Dad next to it,
ruined.

Blue Flower

It's always the same.
And I'm unsure why.

Ivory with a single
blue flower,

darker than your
eyes. My eyes.

A single chip on the handle,
larger than before,

and still, it's your favorite,
and still your poison you pour.

Not large or small,
just right in size

You hold it gently,
perfectly—delicate.

Liquid gold it holds
dear. To your heart,

to your everything,
I pretend not to care.

I'll smash it to smithereens!
I'll smash you too.

Punching, kicking,
crying, I'll make you see, someday.

Your poison kills more than weeds,
feelings—life and you.

The blue flower is wilting
and the ivory fades to gray.

It's still the same and
I fear it will always be,

but your eyes—my eyes.
I can't change. I love you.

I can only smash it
to smithereens.

Your porcelain chalice
that holds what you hold dear.

I wait for my chance,
pretending not to care.

Why

What's in the mug, I wonder—
he stumbles from the room.
Moving close, I hold my breath,
putting my hands over Raggedy Ann's
stitched mouth and triangle nose, fearful
it might do to us what it does to him—
the smelly amber liquid.
I whisper to Ann.
She is quiet, speechless.
Our words have no meaning, mine and Ann's.
Lifeless eyes, unknowing, but we know, we wonder:
Why?

Why drink something
that smells like the cleaner mom uses
in the bathroom?
It takes my breath away when she does.
I stare down into the mug until I must breathe.
I uncover Ann's mouth.
She'll be quiet.
She always is.
She's good, I tell her.

Crash!
I don't flinch.
Neither does Ann.

The rubber tree falls into view,
dirt spilling from the pot.
Then he tries to steady himself
on the door frame.
He trips in my direction but doesn't see me.
Shading Ann's eyes with my hand,
I protect her.
She doesn't like monsters.

Empty eyes of fire and glass,
green like the shaggy rug.
He tries to pat my head,
but misses and hits my ear,
then plops down in his seat,
smiling—pleased with himself.
He drinks it—
the smelly amber liquid.

Blood

Aha! That's it—it's all born of drink.
Turning angels to devils,
saints into sinners,
raise your glasses—*clink clink.*

Warm and burning,
slithering down throats.
Unsaved serpents once human,
their secret uncloaked.

Shapeshifters, the whole lot.
Worthy men turned to stew.
The shared blood between us
I can never undo.

Instructions for Running Away

Shove all my socks deep inside the duffel. The pink one I borrowed from Sam.

Throw open my dresser, *where is my sweater?* It may get cold there—somewhere.

Close my bag, look around my sunshine-colored room, but all I see is darkness.

Sneak out the door, glance back once.

Wish things were different.

Wipe the tears spilling down my cheeks, falling to the mud. I must save myself.

Turn back once more to home, the only one I've known. It looks happy—from the outside.

Wish things were different—that the drinking could stop. It won't.

Run fast and fearful to anywhere but here.

Numb

Blurry, I can't see; I want to be numb.
If only I could sleep more, forever.
My temples pulse loud—the rhythms of a drum.

On the cliff I lay. Then, I see her, and I'm overcome.
I've failed her—them, me. Lord, I surrender.
Blurry, I can't see; I want to be numb.

Sweat and fire—throbbing. I want to be numb.
The sickening smells, my smell. The scent of a beggar.
My temples pulse loud—the rhythms of a drum.

I reach below the cliff; the poison will stop the drums.
Tipping it, *thud*, I look. I beg her,
Blurry, I can't see; I want to be numb.

She's there still, my angel; I need to be numb.
My ragamuffin's arms stretched out, the bottle—I beg.
My temples pulse loud—the rhythms of a drum.

She hands me the glass. I take in the rum.
I reach toward her cheek, chilled like October.
Blurry, I can't see; I want to be numb.

My temples pulse loud—the rhythms of a drum.

Bottom

Falling off the cliff flying, flailing,
Struggling, screaming—reaching.
It's endless
The black hole—
Yours, theirs, ours,
The infected.
No beginning and no end.
Beginnings are made to be forgotten.
None of it matters in the haze and clouds—
blackness with snapshots,
A moment
here and there—click.
A vague recollection of something,
You're unsure what's real.
Spiraling toward something, terrified it's nothing.
When will it end?
The infinite abyss of you.
Lies, hurts, and failures, crushing blows taking your wind
as
you
fall,
Down,
down,
down.
Drowning and choking on murky water, chosen until it chose you,
Tag—you're it.

Here you lie—under it,
The fermented dirt poison rivers from barrels.
Bottoms up—take your medicine.
Cheers—to nothing,
Except for sickness.
The light peeks through the haze—snapshots you sometimes see,
Click.
Let go in the funneling darkness. Stop flailing and close your eyes.
Stop fighting and fall—
Down,
down,
down,
Free.
Take your last sip before the serenity.
Bend your knees to hit first,
Dead stop—crushed!
Shattered into bits—
The bottom, you reached it.
The floor.
The end—the beginning.

I See

Special days are for bacon.
Today is special,
at least she said so.
And she makes the rules.

Crackles and pops—
sound out from the kitchen.
The smell is special,
at least it used to be.

We'd have to leave
by 9:00.
Another cloudy Sunday
for another long drive.

To see him,
take him home.
To have him,
if we ever can.

The car door squeaks
as I climb into my seat,
we ride.
She drives—

excited, nervous, happy, scared.
Her eyes tell the tale—
wide then squinting,
moist and bright.

Bacon sits in my belly,
stiff and unmoving.
Light tears though
the slideshow of trees.

Time ticks—proving things.
The long drive,
we've been here before,
many times.

She thinks this time
My father's different—she always does.
She thinks he might change.
Hope is our destruction.

There he is, she says,
"Go and say hi."
He looks better, alive.
"Hello, Father—hi."

We drive back in silence,
it's always the same.
She wonders if this
is the time he will change.

I see him look
at every passing sign.
Bottles blinking and dimly lit dives,
inviting him.

He looks
not at the light,
tearing through the trees.
He wants—he needs.

I see—waiting, without wonder.
Not anymore.
Time is repetitious,
tick tock tick.

My eyes are the only ones open,
although they burn, sting,
and cry.
It hurts, but I see.

Forever Roots

Woven branches rise to the glorious Sun.
The powerful presence is no longer the perfect shape.
An imperfect symmetry by one bold and rebellious arm.
A child breaking free of her knots—
she fearlessly climbs far away,
on her own.
The others huddle tight, nearly becoming one.
They grow slowly higher toward the breathing sky.
Timid, but relying on each other—
strength.

She runs—unsupported,
enviously they watch her climb.
Free and away, alone on her journey.
Maybe she'll do it—reach the sun,
be part of the moon and stars.
"From roots, we are never free, foolish girl,"
the moon yells down with a laugh.
So close, he seems, but the universe is misleading.

Once daring and flying, now brittle and weak.
She bears no fruit.
She can't go back to them.
She no longer fits.
They wouldn't have her anyway.
She can't grow any more, push any farther.

Dying, breaking—never standing with the stars.
She sobs, falling,
collapsing to the ground.

The powerful presence returns to the perfect shape,
rooted and firm.
The sun bursts through their arms,
woven in unity.
She lays still, lifeless on the ground,
no longer bold or rebellious.
Further still from the moon and stars.
She shuts her eyes to the sun taking her last breath.
She dies—
alone.

Your Children

Every day the battle. It starts on your knees.
Humble, human powerless—you admit,
And that's the start.
We are, too,
powerless.
Over your choices, over it all.
But we won't be forever,
your children.

Every day, the war. You against your desires,
your mistress, your longing.
It beckons—urging you.
You hear it *knock, bang,*
Slam, always there,
simmering, waiting to strike.
In desperation, we hear you scream,
your children.

Helpless to your decision,
we only pray you choose
us—pieces of you,
but that's part of you too,
your liquid lover
who hurts you,
who hurts us.
We won't be forever.
your children

Where do her rivers take you
but away from us.
But you love us,
you say—your children.
Yet there you swim,
into her again, carried away in her current.

But you love us; you say,
disappearing in the waves.
We whisper unheard—your children.

Free Bird

Here on our porch, we sit—
again, by the ocean.
Quiet and close.
The silence rings in my ears.
I wriggle in my seat.
You cross and uncross your legs.
I've begged and prayed
for this quiet—
this peace.

You've worked for it,
hard.
Memories of chaos
slip away.
Yours are hazy, saturated in substance.
Mine lie dormant but will awaken.
Biting, springing from comfort,
ready for war.
If there is a reason.
If he gives me one.

We are still, strange, and uncomfortable,
settling into predictability.
A new father and daughter.
The old memories.

Smoke from your cigarette flies away in the wind.
I envision myself dissolving into vapor,
flying away with it—free,
away from here.

I'd like to scream.
You look about to burst—Or drink.
It's all that we've wanted.
All that we've asked for—Normal.
Like the others,
the ones not possessed, obsessed—
the free birds.

Without it, we thought we could be
normal—
Like them.
But we're not, and now we know it.
Sober but never escaping.
Never a free bird.
Never them.

When You Died

Life keeps moving, but ours remains still,
and there is silence in every sound.
Your musky scent fades, but I sometimes smell you close.
Your smile falls away,
and I sleep another night,
forgetting you.
And I wake another morning,
trying to remember.
What's left of us crumbles to pieces,
but were we ever whole?
Your wife, son, and daughter,
missing a father—
missing you.

Down, down, down,
the man's voice repeats in my mediation.
Going deeper now, freeing myself from anxiety,
over the loss of you, over the years with you.
We fall to pieces, but were we ever whole?
We no longer have a purpose.
Were you our reason?
Your sickness and your health,
twisted vows unknowingly taken
in commitment to your disease.
We waited on your decision,
sober or drunk.
Every day was new.

Going deeper now,
down, down, down.
Freeing myself from you, but never forgetting.
While losing us, the rest of us, what's left of us,
wife, son, and daughter,
breaking in pieces,
down, down, down.
Your scent, I can no longer smell.
Everything moves but is still, and the sounds are stills silent
Will I ever be whole?
Was I ever—where we?
You fly away in the wind like the musk,
away from what's left—there's nothing left.

Our Authors

Funnel To Freedoms Ring By Andre Brewer
Its Not About You By Jeremiah Valentine
Soft Reflection By Jamie Lim
Hashra By Abinash Singh Chib
Where Have All The Bluejays Gone By Jennifer Ayala
Sunlight Reflector By Sarah Cross
Whispers In The Wind By Echo Quinn
Questions We Didn't Ask Out Loud By Mars Hetherson
Walking Through The Four Seasons By Eugene Stelzig
Serving Sweet Tea By Lisa Kendrick
Dispelling The Clouds By Rivka Conway
Summers In Laurel Canyon By Spencer J. Vigil
Burnout By Jeff Kimball
Whispers of Daydreams By April Federico
Unheard Whispers By Dianne C. Braley
MuVik By Munawwar Sharifi

CPSIA information can be obtained
at www.ICGtesting.com
Printed in the USA
LVHW081312020422
714993LV00012BA/760